SWEENEY'S FLIGHT

BASED ON THE REVISED TEXT OF
'SWEENEY ASTRAY'
SEAMUS HEANEY

PHOTOGRAPHS BY
RACHEL GIESE

——

WITH THE COMPLETE
REVISED TEXT OF
'SWEENEY ASTRAY'

——

faber and faber

Sweeney's Flight first published in Great Britain in 1992
by Faber and Faber Limited
3 Queen Square London WC1N 3AU

Sweeney Astray first published in Ireland in 1983
by Field Day Theatre Company, Derry
First published in Great Britain in 1984
by Faber and Faber Limited
Published with revisions in this edition in 1992

Photoset by Wilmaset Ltd, Wirral
Printed in England by Jolly and Barber, Rugby, Warks

Seamus Heaney is hereby identified as author of this work
in accordance with Section 77
of the Copyright, Designs and Patents Act 1988

A CIP record for this book
is available from the British Library

ISBN 0-571-16015-8

The poem 'The King of the Ditchbacks' by Seamus Heaney
is from *Station Island*, Faber and Faber Ltd, 1984

Contents

Preface by Seamus Heaney   vii

Photographer's acknowledgements   ix

I   SWEENEY'S FLIGHT
Text and photographs   1
List of photographs   82

II   SWEENEY ASTRAY
Introduction   87
Notes and acknowledgements   89
Revised text 1992   91

Preface

Long before the idea of *Sweeney's Flight* emerged, Rachel Giese had been spending time in Ireland, photographing the country around Errigal in County Donegal. This resulted in her collaborating on a book with Cathal Ó Searcaigh, a native of the area who writes in the Irish language and whose collection of poems was called *Súile Shuibhne* (meaning 'Sweeney's Eyes'); but even if the name had never been mentioned, the photographs in that book and in her subsequent *The Donegal Pictures* (1988) would have convinced me that Rachel Giese was the person to look again at Sweeney's places as they are identified in *Sweeney Astray* and to represent them from her own particular perspective.

Over the years there had been a number of different proposals to do a book like this one, using my own poems as a supplement or a stimulus for the pictures; yet even though these proposals came from people whose work I knew and admired, I never felt ready to go ahead with the project. My reluctance had to do with an unease about the problematic relation between image and text. I always shied from the combination of speechless photograph and wordlogged verse: I think I felt that in these cases (to be extreme about it) the photograph was absolute and the text a pretext. This was more a hesitation than a conviction: all I can say is that I tended to foresee misalliance of some sort between the impersonal, instantaneous thereness of the picture on one side of the page, and the personal, time-stretching pleas of the verse on the other.

The Sweeney stanzas, however, constitute a different case. This material belongs to everyone, it has the given, anonymous in-placeness of hillsides and shorelines, and even though it dramatizes the predicament of an individual character, the character himself is often less an individual than a mouthpiece for the common, primary sensations and emotions which everybody experiences in the presence of the natural world. Indeed, in making the selection of verse which here accompanies Rachel Giese's photographs, I was indulging in a pleasure I had denied myself when I first approached the task of translating *Buile Suibhne* twenty years ago. My original desire had been to snatch certain moments of definition and intensity out of their place in the story and to present them as lyric poems in their own right, but in the end I felt this would have been too high-handed a treatment. Nevertheless, the hankering to skim off certain favourite lines persisted, and when I saw Rachel's pictures, I realized that the right person had arrived at the right time. I was immediately emboldened to snip lyric leaves off the old narrative boughs.

Once we had decided to go ahead with the project, Rachel Giese and I proceeded separately to accumulate our different contributions. Over a number of years Rachel kept returning to Co. Antrim and other parts of Ulster lying within and beyond the boundaries of Sweeney's original kingdom of Dal-Arie. She felt at home there anyhow. As she took her pictures, she did not have any specific illustrative purpose in mind but was allowing herself to be drawn to places and atmospheres which she felt to be in tune with her recollections of the poetry.

Similarly, as I drifted through the text in search of bits that might stand on their own, I made the selection not according to any 'visual' quotient in the lines, but because of their inherent possibilities as independent lyric poems. And then, once I began the actual business of extracting stanzas, I was tempted into little acts of revision. For one thing, there is a slightly different rhythmic imperative in operation when a piece stands on its own than when it is a constituent element in some longer structure. And besides, in the case of translation, it is even truer than usual that a poem is never completed, merely abandoned. So the lines that I eventually orphaned from the story often differed in several minor instances from the lines as they appear in other printings of *Sweeney Astray*; and these changes, as well as a number of others I made in lines that do not appear alongside the photographs, necessitated the inclusion in this volume of a new edition of the whole translation.

It was felt, moreover, that the introduction which appeared in the first edition should be retained for the benefit of readers encountering the work here for the first time, so it has been reprinted with the revised text. The volume begins, however, with a poem which evolved from my experience of translating *Buile Suibhne* in the first place. 'The King of the Ditchbacks' is a triptych, of which the first part was written a year or two before I thought of undertaking the work at all. In retrospect, it seems as if Sweeney had already arrived and was presenting his visiting card: the 'trespasser' moving behind the hedges was simply biding his time. And, when his time came, I proceeded into the paths of absorption and 'migrant solitude' which the other two sections of the poem attempt to evoke.

S.H.

Photographer's Acknowledgements

In the six-year quest for Sweeney's haunts many people aided and comforted me, luring me out of hail-storms and thorny trees into the warmth of their homes, or sometimes pointing me to thornier, rockier places.

My thanks go to the Community and staff of the Servite Priory, Benburb, Co. Tyrone; the staff of the Tyrone Guthrie Arts Centre, Annaghmakerrig, Co. Monaghan; Lance and Susan Wright, James and Alanna Boyle, Tony and Clare Eklof, Noelle and Gerry Smullen; to Basil Lenaghan for tree identifications; and special thanks to Cathal Ó Searcaigh for years of friendship, learning and insight.

To my father Slater Brown, who generously contributed to the completion of this work, and to Graham Giese, who has lovingly supported this and all my work, goes my deepest gratitude.

R.G.

I

SWEENEY'S FLIGHT

The King of the Ditchbacks

As if a trespasser
unbolted a forgotten gate
and ripped the growth
tangling its lower bars —

just beyond the hedge
he has opened a dark morse
along the bank,
a crooked wounding

of silent, cobwebbed
grass. If I stop
he stops
like the moon.

He lives in his feet
and ears, weather-eyed,
all pad and listening,
a denless mover.

Under the bridge
his reflection shifts
sideways to the current,
mothy, alluring.

I am haunted
by his stealthy rustling,
the unexpected spoor,
the pollen settling.

II

I was sure I knew him. The time I'd spent obsessively in that upstairs room bringing myself close to him: each entranced hiatus as I chainsmoked and stared out the dormer into the grassy hillside I was laying myself open. He was depending on me as I hung out on the limb of a translated phrase like a youngster dared out on to an alder branch over the whirlpool. Small dreamself in the branches. Dream fears I inclined towards, interrogating:

— Are you the one I ran upstairs to find drowned under running water in the bath?
— The one the mowing machine severed like a hare in the stiff frieze of harvest?
— Whose little bloody clothes we buried in the garden?
— The one who lay awake in darkness a wall's breadth from the troubled hoofs?

After I had dared these invocations, I went back towards the gate to follow him. And my stealth was second nature to me, as if I were coming into my own. I remembered I had been vested for this calling.

III

When I was taken aside that day
I had the sense of election:

they dressed my head in a fishnet
and plaited leafy twigs through meshes

so my vision was a bird's
at the heart of a thicket

and I spoke as I moved
like a voice from a shaking bush.

King of the ditchbacks,
I went with them obediently

to the edge of a pigeon wood —
deciduous canopy, screened wain of evening

we lay beneath in silence.
No birds came, but I waited

among briars and stones, or whispered
or broke the watery gossamers

if I moved a muscle.
'Come back to us,' they said, 'in harvest,

when we hide in the stooked corn,
when the gundogs can hardly retrieve

what's brought down.' And I saw myself
rising to move in that dissimulation,

top-knotted, masked in sheaves, noting
the fall of birds: a rich young man

leaving everything he had
for a migrant solitude.

for John Montague

'All [Fh]arannain, adhbha náomh,
co n-iomad call caomh is cnúas,
uisge tinnesnach can tess
ag snige re a chness anúas.

As iomdha ann eidhnech ghlass
agus meass re mberar geall
agus abhall chenntrom chaomh
ag filliudh a craobh fa cheann.

Imdha broc ag dol fa a dhíon,
ann is miol muighe nach mall,
is édan rionntanach róin
ag techt on muir moir anall.

Me Suibhne mac Colmáin chóir,
mor n-oidhchi reoidh bhim co fann,
romthruaill Rónán do Druim Gess,
codlaim fa chraoibh 'san ess tall.' All.

[I]

Sainted cliff at Alternan,
nut grove, hazel-wood!
Cold quick sweeps of water
fall down the cliff-side.

Ivies green and thicken there,
its oak-mast is precious.
Fruited branches nod and bend
from heavy-headed apple trees.

Badgers make their setts there
and swift hares have their form;
and seals' heads swim the ocean,
cobbling the running foam.

And by the waterfall, Colman's son,
Ronan of Drumgesh's victim,
haggard, spent, frost-bitten Sweeney,
is sleeping at the foot of a tree.

[11]

A year until last night
I have lived among dark trees,
between the flood and ebb-tide,
going cold and naked

with no pillow for my head,
no human company
and, so help me, God,
no spear and no sword.

No surge of royal blood,
camped here in solitude;
no glory flames the wood,
no friends, no music.

Tell the truth: a hard lot.
And no shirking this fate;
no sleep, no respite,
no hope for a long time.

No house, humming full,
no men, loud with good will,
nobody to call me king,
no drink or banqueting.

No skilled musicians' cunning,
no soft discoursing women,
no open-handed giving;
my doom to be a long dying.

Our sorrows were multiplied
that Tuesday when Congal fell.
Our dead made a great harvest,
our remnant, a last swathe.

This has been my plight.
Fallen from noble heights,
grieving and astray,
a year until last night.

[III]

Tonight the snow is cold.
I was at the end of my tether
but hunger and bother
are endless.

Look at me, broken
and down-at-heel,
Sweeney from Rasharkin.
Look at me now,

wind-scourged, stripped
like a winter tree
clad in black frost
and frozen snow.

Hard grey branches
have torn my hands,
the skin of my feet
is in strips from briars

and the pain of frostbite
has put me astray,
from Slemish to Slieve Gullion,
from Slieve Gullion to Cooley.

I went raving with grief
on the top of Croagh Patrick,
from Glen Bolcain to Islay,
from Kintyre to Mourne.

I woke at dawn
with a fasting spittle:
then at Cloonkill, a bunch of cress,
then at Kilnoo, the cuckoo flower.

I wish I lived safe
and sound in Rasharkin
and not here, heartbroken,
in my bare pelt, at bay in snow.

[IV]

I spent a whole year on the mountain
enduring my transformation,
dabbing, dabbing like a bird
at the holly berry's crimson.

19]

[v]

From the well at Druim Crib, watercress
supplies my bit and sup at terce;
its juices that have greened my chin
are Sweeney's markings and birth-stain.

[VI]

I perched for rest and imagined
cuckoos calling across water,
the Bann cuckoo, calling sweeter
than church bells that whinge and grind.

From the crag of Lough Diolar
up to Derry Colmcille
I saw great swans and heard their calls
sweetly rebuking wars and battles.

On solitary cliffs, a stag
bells and makes the whole glen shake
and re-echo. I am ravished.
Unearthly sweetness shakes my breast.

O Christ, the loving and the sinless,
hear my prayer, attend, O Christ,
and let nothing separate us.
Blend me forever in your sweetness.

[VII]

The harper who harped me to rest,
where is his soothing music now?
My people too, my kith and kin,
where did their affection go?

Fugitive, deserted, mocked
by memories of my days as king,
no longer called to head the troop
when warriors are mustering,

no longer the guest of honour
at tables anywhere in Ireland,
ranging like a mad pilgrim
over rock-peaks on the mountain.

[VIII]

Woods and forests and wild deer –
things like these delight you more
than sleeping in your eastern dun
on a bed of feather-down.

Near a quick mill-pond, your perch
on a dark green holly branch
means far more now than any feast
among the brightest and the best.

[IX]

Gazing down at clean gravel,
to lean out over a cool well,
drink a mouthful of sunlit water
and gather cress by the handful.

27]

[X]

I imagine treelines
far away,
a banked-up, soothing
wooded haze.

[XI]

The bushy leafy oak tree
is highest in the wood,
the forking shoots of hazel
hide sweet hazel-nuts.

The alder is my darling,
all thornless in the gap,
some milk of human kindness
coursing in its sap.

The blackthorn is a jaggy creel
stippled with dark sloes;
green watercress in thatch on wells
where the drinking blackbird goes.

Sweetest of the leafy stalks,
the vetches strew the pathway;
the oyster-grass is my delight,
and the wild strawberry.

Low-set clumps of apple trees
drum down fruit when shaken;
scarlet berries clot like blood
on mountain rowan.

Briars curl in sideways,
arch a stickle back,
draw blood and curl up innocent
to sneak the next attack.

The yew tree in each churchyard
wraps night in its dark hood.
Ivy is a shadowy
genius of the wood.

Holly rears its windbreak,
a door in winter's face;
life-blood on a spear-shaft
darkens the grain of ash.

Birch tree, smooth and blessed,
delicious to the breeze,
high twigs plait and crown it
the queen of trees.

The aspen pales
and whispers, hesitates:
a thousand frightened scuts
race in its leaves.

But what disturbs me most
in the leafy wood
is the to and fro and to and fro
of an oak rod.

35]

[XII]

I love the ancient ivy tree,
the pale-leafed sallow,
the birch's sibilant melody,
the solemn yew.

37]

[XIII]

I would live happy
in an ivy bush
high in some twisted tree
and never come out.

The skylarks rising
into their high space
send me pitching and tripping
over stumps on the moor

and my hurry flushes
the turtle-dove.
I overtake it,
my plumage rushing,

am startled then
by the startled woodcock
or a blackbird's sudden
volubility.

I prefer the scurry
and song of blackbirds
to the usual blather
of men and women.

I prefer the squeal of badgers
in their sett
to the hullabuloo
of the morning hunt.

I prefer the re-
echoing belling of a stag
among the peaks
to that terrible horn.

[XIV]

Without bed or board
I face dark days
in frozen lairs
and wind-driven snow.

Ice scoured by winds.
Watery shadows from weak sun.
Shelter from the one tree
on a plateau.

Haunting deerpaths,
enduring rain,
first-footing the grey
frosted grass.

I climb towards the pass
and the stag's belling
rings off the wood,
surf-noise rises

where I go, heartbroken
and worn out,
sharp-haunched Sweeney,
raving and moaning.

[XV]

A starry frost will come
dropping on the pools
and I'll be out
on unsheltered hills:

herons calling
in cold Glenelly,
flocks of birds quickly
coming and going.

45]

[XVI]

I gather cress
in delicious bunches,
four round handfuls
in Glen Bolcain;

and then I unpick
the shy bog-berry,
then drink water
from Ronan's well.

My nails are bent,
my loins weak,
my feet bleeding,
my thighs bare.

[XVII]

I need woods
for consolation,
some grove in Meath –
or the space of Ossory.

Or Ulster in harvest.
Strangford, shimmering.
Or a summer visit
to green Tyrone.

At Lammas I migrate
to the pools of Teltown,
pass the springtime fishing
bends of the Shannon.

I often get as far
as my old domain,
those groomed armies,
those stern hillsides.

49]

[XVIII]

Ailsa Craig,
the seagulls' home,
God knows it is
hard lodgings.

Ailsa Craig,
bell-shaped rock,
reaching sky-high,
snout in the sea –

it hard-beaked,
me seasoned and scraggy:
we mated like a couple
of hard-shanked cranes.

[XIX]

One night I walked across the Fews –
the hills were dark, the starlight dead –
when suddenly five severed heads,
five lantern ghouls, appeared and rose

like bats from hell, surrounding me.
Then a head spoke – another shock!
– This is the Ulster lunatic.
Let us drive him into the sea!

I went like an arrow from a bow.
My feet disdained that upland ground.
Goat-head and dog-head cursed but found
me impossible to follow.

[XX]

I have deserved all this:
night-vigils, terror,
flittings across water,
women's cried-out eyes.

[XXI]

My life is steady lamentation.
The roof above my head has gone.
I am doomed to rags, starved and mad,
brought to this by the power of God.

Going drenched in teems of rain,
crouching under thunderstorms.
Summering where herons stalk.
Wintering out among wolf-packs.

59]

[XXII]

In November, wild ducks fly.
From those dark evenings until May
let us forage, nest and hide
in ivy in the brown-floored wood

and hear behind the late birds' song
sounds of water in Glen Bolcain,
its streams, all hurry, hush and jabber,
its islands in the forking rivers,

its hazel trees and holly bowers,
its leaves, its acorns and its briars,
its nuts, its sharp-tasting sloes,
all its cool-fleshed winter berries;

and under trees, its hounds coursing,
its dappled antlered stags belling,
its water's endless, endless fall –
sounds of water in Glen Bolcain.

[XXIII]

Almighty God, I deserved this,
my cut feet, my drained face,
winnowed by a sheer wind
and miserable in my mind.

Last night I lay in Mourne
plastered in wet; cold rain poured.
Tonight, in torment, in Glasgally
I am crucified in the fork of a tree.

I who endured unflinchingly
through long nights and long days
since the feathers penned my frame
foresee nothing but the same.

Hard weather has withered me,
blizzards have buried me.
As I wince here in cutting wind
Glen Bolcain's heather haunts my mind.

All this is hard to thole, Lord!
Still without bed or board,
crouching to graze on cress,
drinking cold water from rivers.

Alarmed out of the autumn wood,
whipped by whins, flecked with blood,
running wild among wolf-packs,
shying away with the red stag.

Son of God, have mercy on us!
Never to hear a human voice!
To sleep naked every night
up there in the highest thickets,

to have lost my proper shape and looks,
a mad scuttler on mountain peaks,
a derelict doomed to loneliness:
Son of God, have mercy on us!

[XXIV]

If I show my heels
I am hobbled by guilt.
I am a sheep
without a fold.

[XXV]

Every night I glean and raid
and comb the floor of the oak wood.
My hands work into leaf and rind,
old roots, old windfalls on the ground,

they rake through matted watercress
and grope among the bog-berries,
cool brooklime, sorrel and damp moss,
wild garlic and wild raspberries,

apples, hazelnuts and acorns,
the haws of sharp, jaggy hawthorns,
the blackberries, the floating weed,
the whole store of the oak wood.

[XXVI]

There was a time when I preferred
the turtle-dove's soft jubilation
as it flitted round a pool
to the murmur of conversation.

There was a time when I preferred
the blackbird singing on the hill
and the stag loud against the storm
to the clinking tongue of this bell.

There was a time when I preferred
the mountain grouse crying at dawn
to the voice and closeness
of a beautiful woman.

There was a time when I preferred
wolf-packs yelping and howling
to the sheepish voice of a cleric
bleating out plainsong.

You are welcome to pledge healths
and carouse in your drinking dens;
I will dip and steal water
from a well with my open palm.

You are welcome to that cloistered hush
of your students' conversation;
I will study the pure chant
of hounds baying in Glen Bolcain.

You are welcome to your salt meat
and fresh meat in feasting-houses;
I will live content elsewhere
on tufts of green watercress.

The herd's sharp spear wounded me
and passed clean through my body.
Ah Christ, who disposed all things, why
was I not killed at Moira?

Of all the innocent lairs I made
the length and breadth of Ireland
I remember an open bed
above the lough in Mourne.

Of all the innocent lairs I made
the length and breadth of Ireland
I remember bedding down
above the wood in Glen Bolcain.

To You, Christ, I give thanks
for Your Body in communion.
Whatever evil I have done
in this world, I repent.

[XXVII]

The springs I always liked
were the fountain at Dunmall
and the spring-well on Knocklayde
that tasted pure and cool.

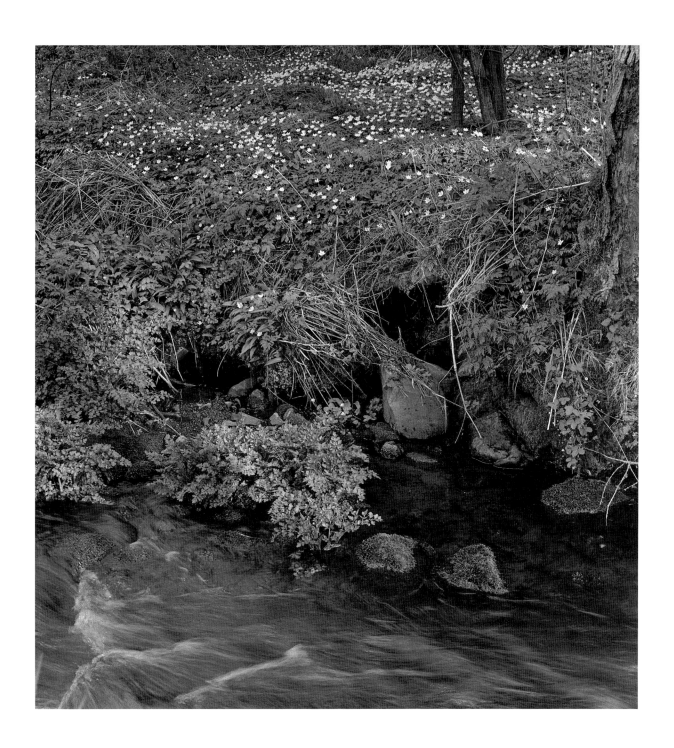

[XXVIII]

I am standing beside Sweeney's grave
remembering him. Wherever he
loved and nested and removed to
will always be dear to me.

Because Sweeney loved Glen Bolcain,
I learned to love it too. He'll miss
all the fresh streams tumbling down,
all the beds of watercress.

He would drink his sup of water from
the well beyond that we have called
The Madman's Well: and now his name
keeps brimming in its sandy cold.

Because Mad Sweeney was a pilgrim
to the lip of every well
and every green-banked, cress-topped stream,
their water's his memorial.

I ask a blessing, by Sweeney's grave.
His memory rises in my breast.
His soul roosts in the tree of love.
His body sinks in its clay nest.

THE PHOTOGRAPHS

page   i *Frontispiece*: Mist near Muckish
         3 Door in abandoned orchard (*detail of page* 81)
         7 Solitary apple, clouds
        11 Waterfall at Kenbane
        17 Nest in snowy thorn
        19 Thorns (Nosegay for Sweeney)
        21 Broken reflection in pool
        23 Errigal and Little Errigal
           reflected in Lough Gaineamh
        27 Watercress and grasses
        29 Sunrise in wood by the Blackwater
        31 Leaning grove
        35 Wood sorrel in slanting light
        37 Birch and vines
        41 Rooks
        43 Lone tree on Antrim plain
        45 Frost on thistle
        47 Raindrops on pool
        49 Slemish, cashel, pole
        51 Cliffs at Dunseverick
        53 Road to Errigal
        54 Rocks in Poisoned Glen
        56 Rathlin coast
        57 Moonlight on Lough Altan
        59 Aghla Mór in hailstorm
        61 River in spate
        63 Bend in the Blackwater
        66 Rock face
        67 Leaning rock
        69 Trees at Tobermason
        71 Apple tree
        73 Sheep in snow and mist
        77 Wood anemone by stream
        79 Errigal, daybreak
        81 Door
        83 Sheep's skull

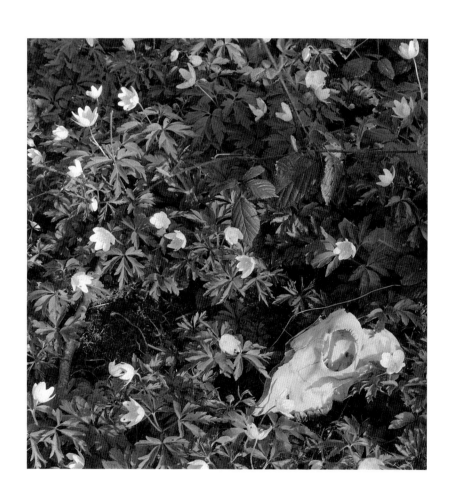

II

SWEENEY ASTRAY

revised 1992

Introduction

This version of *Buile Suibhne* is based on J. G. O'Keeffe's bilingual edition, which was published by the Irish Texts Society in 1913. In the meantime, Flann O'Brien gave its central character a second life, as hilarious as it was melancholy, when he made Sweeney part of the apparatus of his novel *At Swim-Two-Birds*; and a number of other poets and scholars have continued to make translations of different sections of the verse.

The basis of the 1913 edition is a manuscript written in County Sligo between 1671 and 1674. This manuscript is part of the Stowe collection in the Royal Irish Academy and O'Keeffe believed that, on linguistic grounds, 'the text might have been composed at any time between the years 1200 and 1500'. Nevertheless, the thing was already taking shape in the ninth century. O'Keeffe cites a reference in the *Book of Aicill*, a text dating from the tenth century at the latest, to stories and poems relating to Sweeney's madness; and other evidence from literary and historical sources leads him to conclude that the *Buile Suibhne* which we now possess is a development of traditions dating back to the time of the Battle of Moira (AD 637), the battle where Sweeney went mad and was transformed, in fulfilment of St Ronan's curse, into a creature of the air.

What we have, then, is a literary creation; unlike Finn McCool or Cuchulain, Sweeney is not a given figure of myth or legend but an historically situated character, although the question of whether he is based upon an historical king called Sweeney has to remain an open one. But the literary imagination which fastened upon him as an image was clearly in the grip of a tension between the newly dominant Christian ethos and the older, recalcitrant Celtic temperament. The opening sections which recount the collision between the peremptory ecclesiastic and the sacral king, and the closing pages of uneasy reconciliation set in St Moling's monastery, are the most explicit treatment of this recurrent theme. This alone makes the work a significant one, but it does not exhaust its significance. For example, insofar as Sweeney is also a figure of the artist, displaced, guilty, assuaging himself by his utterance, it is possible to read the work as an aspect of the quarrel between free creative imagination and the constraints of religious, political, and domestic obligation. It is equally possible, in a more opportunistic spirit, to dwell upon Sweeney's easy sense of cultural affinity with both western Scotland and southern Ireland as exemplary for all men and women in contemporary Ulster, or to ponder the thought that this Irish invention may well have been a development of a British original, vestigially present in the tale of the madman called Alan (Sections 46–50).

But the work makes its immediate claims more by its local power to affect us than by any general implications we may discover in its pattern. We have to go to *King Lear*, to Edgar's jabbering masquerade as Poor Tom – itself an interesting parallel to Sweeney's condition – to find poetry as piercingly exposed to the beauties and severities of the natural world. We may even want to go back further, to the hard weather of the Anglo-Saxon 'Seafarer', or (in order to match the occasional opposite moods of jubilation) to the praise poetry of the early Irish hermits. It was the bareness and durability of the writing here, its double note of relish and penitence, that first tempted me to try my hand at translating it and gave me the encouragement to persist with stretches of less purely inspired quatrains.

My first impulse had been to forage for the best lyric moments and to present them as poetic orphans, out of the context of the story. These points of poetic intensity, rather than the overall organization of the narrative, establish the work's highest artistic levels and offer the strongest invitations to the translator of verse. Yet I gradually felt I had to earn the right to do the high points by undertaking the whole thing: what I was dealing with, after all, is a major work in the canon of medieval literature.

Nevertheless, a small number of the original stanzas have been excluded (see Notes, page 89). I occasionally abbreviated the linking narrative and in places have used free verse to render the more heightened prose passages. O'Keeffe has been my guide to the interpretation of the line-by-line meaning, though I have now and again invested the poems with a more subjective tone than they possess in Irish. The stanza forms employed do not reflect the syllabic and assonantal disciplines of the original metres, but since the work could be regarded as a primer of lyric genres – laments, dialogues, litanies, rhapsodies, curses – I trust that the variety of dramatic pitch in the English will compensate to some extent for the loss of the metrical satisfactions in the Irish.

My fundamental relation with Sweeney, however, is topographical. His kingdom lay in what is now south County Antrim and north County Down, and for over thirty years I lived on the verges of that territory, in sight of some of Sweeney's places and in earshot of others – Slemish, Rasharkin, Benevenagh, Dunseverick, the Bann, the Roe, the Mournes. When I began work on this version, I had just moved to Wicklow, not all that far from Sweeney's final resting ground at St Mullins. I was in a country of woods and hills and remembered that the green spirit of the hedges embodied in Sweeney had first been embodied for me in the persons of a family of tinkers, also called Sweeney, who used to camp in the ditch-backs along the road to the first school I attended. One way or another, he seemed to have been with me from the start.

S.H.

Notes and Acknowledgements

The sections of the text are numbered to correspond with J. G. O'Keeffe's divisions in the Irish Texts Society edition.

Six stanzas have been dropped from Section 16, seven from Section 40, and one from Section 43. In the first case, the material omitted is historical allusion; in the second, obscurity defeated ingenuity; and in the third, I felt that the English poem came to rest better at the penultimate stanza.

Section 82 and the first fifteen stanzas of Section 83 have also been excluded. There an exchange occurs between Moling, Mongan, and Sweeney which is essentially a recapitulation and seemed to me to impede the momentum of the conclusion.

I have anglicized the name of Sweeney's kingdom, Dal Araidhe, to Dal-Arie, and in dealing with other place names have followed the suggestions in O'Keeffe's notes and index. In the following cases, where no help was offered, I took the liberty of inventing my own equivalents of the Irish: Kilreagan, Cloonkill, Kilnoo, Drumfree, Drumduff, Kilsooney, Doovey, Creegaille, Glasgally.

I am grateful for various encouragements and assistances offered by the late Dr Deirdre Flanagan, Henry Pearson, Colin Middleton, and An t-Ollamh Breandán S. MacAodha.

Sweeney Astray

1 We have already told how Sweeney, son of Colman Cuar and king of Dal-Arie, went astray when he flew out of the battle. This story tells the why and the wherefore of his fits and trips, why he of all men was subject to such frenzies; and it also tells what happened to him afterwards.

2 There was a certain Ronan Finn in Ireland, a holy and distinguished cleric. He was ascetic and pious, an active missionary, a real Christian soldier. He was a worthy servant of God, one who punished his body for the good of his soul, a shield against vice and the devil's attacks, a gentle, genial, busy man.

3 One time when Sweeney was king of Dal-Arie, Ronan was there marking out a church called Killaney. Sweeney was in a place where he heard the clink of Ronan's bell as he was marking out the site, so he asked his people what the sound was.

– It is Ronan Finn, son of Bearach, they said. He is marking out a church in your territory and what you hear is the ringing of his bell.

Sweeney was suddenly angered and rushed away to hunt the cleric from the church. Eorann, his wife, a daughter of Conn of Ciannacht, tried to hold him back and snatched at the fringe of his crimson cloak, but the silver cloak-fastener broke at the shoulder and sprang across the room. She got the cloak all right but Sweeney had bolted, stark naked, and soon landed with Ronan.

4 He found the cleric glorifying the King of heaven and earth, in full voice in front of his psalter, a beautiful illuminated book. Sweeney grabbed the book and flung it into the cold depths of a lake nearby, where it sank without trace. Then he took hold of Ronan and was dragging him out through the church when he heard a cry of alarm. The call came from a servant of Congal Claon's who had come with orders from Congal to summon Sweeney to battle at Moira. He gave a full report of the business and Sweeney went off directly with the servant, leaving the cleric distressed at the loss of his psalter and smarting from such contempt and abuse.

5 A day and a night passed and then an otter rose out of the lake with the psalter and brought it to Ronan, completely unharmed. Ronan gave thanks to God for that miracle, and cursed Sweeney, saying:

6   Sweeney has trespassed upon me,
    abused me sacrilegiously
    and laid violent hands upon me
    to drag me with him from Killaney.

    When Sweeney heard my bell ringing
    he came all of a sudden hurtling,
    raving and raging wild against me
    to drive me off and banish me.

    Insult like that – being thrown
    off ground that I had marked and chosen –
    was too grievous to endure;
    so God inclined unto my prayer.

    My hand was locked in Sweeney's hand
    until he heard a loud command:
    he was called to Moira, bid to join
    battle with Donal on the plain.

    And so I offered thanks and praise
    for the grace of my release,
    that unpredictable off-chance
    of marching orders from the prince.

    From far off he approached the field
    that drove his mind and senses wild.
    He shall roam Ireland, mad and bare.
    He shall find death on the point of a spear.

    The psalter that he grabbed and tore
    from me and cast into deep water –
    Christ brought it back without a spot.
    The psalter stayed immaculate.

    A day and a night in brimming waters,
    my speckled book was none the worse!

Through the will of God the Son
an otter gave me it again.

This psalter that he profaned
I bequeath with a malediction:
that it bode evil for Colman's race
the day this psalter meets their eyes.

Bare to the world, here came Sweeney
to harass and to harrow me:
therefore, it is God's decree
bare to the world he'll always be.

Eorann, daughter of Conn of Ciannacht,
tried to hold him by his cloak.
Eorann has my blessing for this
but Sweeney lives under my curse.

7 After that, Ronan came to Moira to make peace
between Donal, son of Aodh, and Congal Claon, son
of Scannlan, but he did not succeed. Nevertheless,
the cleric's presence was taken as a seal and guaran-
tee of the rules of the battle; they made agreements
that no killing would be allowed except between those
hours they had set for beginning and ending the fight
each day. Sweeney, however, would continually violate every peace and truce which the cleric had
ratified, slaying a man each day before the sides were
engaged and slaying another each evening when the
combat was finished. Then, on the day fixed for the
great battle, Sweeney was in the field before everyone
else.

8 He was dressed like this:
next his white skin, the shimmer of silk;
and his satin girdle around him;
and his tunic, that reward of service
and gift of fealty from Congal,
was like this –
crimson, close-woven,
bordered in gemstones and gold,
a rustle of sashes and loops,
the studded silver gleaming,
the slashed hem embroidered in points.
He had an iron-shod spear in each hand,
a shield of mottled horn on his back,
a gold-hilted sword at his side.

9 He marched out like that until he encountered Ronan
with eight psalmists from his community. They were
blessing the armies, sprinkling them with holy water,
and they sprinkled Sweeney with the rest. Sweeney
thought they had done it just to mock him, so he lifted
one of his spears, hurled it, and killed one of Ronan's
psalmists in a single cast. He made another throw
with the second spear at the cleric himself, so that it
pierced the bell that hung from his neck, and the shaft
sprang off into the air. Ronan burst out:

10   My curse fall on Sweeney
for his great offence.
His smooth spear profaned
my bell's holiness,

cracked bell hoarding grace
since the first saint rang it –
it will curse you to the trees,
bird-brain among branches.

Just as the spear-shaft broke
and sprang into the air
may the mad spasms strike
you, Sweeney, forever.

My fosterling lies slain,
your spear-point has been reddened:
to finish off this bargain
you shall die at spear-point.

Should the steadfast tribe of Owen
try to oppose me,
Uradhran and Telle
will visit them with decay.

Uradhran and Telle
have visited them with decay.
Until time dies away
my curse attend you.

My blessing upon Eorann,
that she flourish and grow lovely.
Through everlasting pain
my curse fall on Sweeney.

11 There were three great shouts as the herded armies
clashed and roared out their war cries like stags.
When Sweeney heard these howls and echoes

assumed into the travelling clouds and amplified through the vaults of space, he looked up and he was possessed by a dark rending energy.

> His brain convulsed,
> his mind split open.
> Vertigo, hysteria, lurchings
> and launchings came over him,
> he staggered and flapped desperately,
> he was revolted by the thought of known places
> and dreamed strange migrations.
> His fingers stiffened,
> his feet scuffled and flurried,
> his heart was startled,
> his senses were mesmerized,
> his sight was bent,
> the weapons fell from his hands
> and he levitated in a frantic cumbersome motion
> like a bird of the air.
> And Ronan's curse was fulfilled.

12 His feet skimmed over the grasses so lightly he never unsettled a dewdrop and all that day he was a hurtling visitant of plain and field, bare mountain and bog, thicket and marshland, and there was no hill or hollow, no plantation or forest in Ireland that he did not appear in that day; until he reached Ros Bearaigh in Glen Arkin, where he hid in a yew tree in the glen.

13 Donal, son of Aodh, won the battle that day. A kinsman of Sweeney's called Aongus the Stout survived and came fleeing with a band of his people into Glen Arkin. They were wondering about Sweeney because they had not seen him alive after the fight and he had not been counted among the casualties. They were discussing this and deciding that Ronan's curse had something to do with it when Sweeney spoke out of the yew:

14 Soldiers, come here.
You are from Dal-Arie,
and the man you are looking for
roosts in his tree.

The life God grants me now
is bare and strait;
I am haggard, womanless,
and cut off from music.

So I am here at Ros Bearaigh.
Ronan has brought me low,
God has exiled me from myself –
soldiers, forget the man you knew.

15 When the men heard Sweeney's recitation they knew him at once and tried to persuade him to trust them. He said he never would, and as they closed round the tree, he launched himself nimbly and lightly and flew to Kilreagan in Tyrconnell, where he perched on the old tree by the church.

It turned out that Donal, son of Aodh, and his army were there after the battle, and when they saw the madman lighting in the tree, a crowd of them ringed and besieged it. They began shouting out guesses about the creature in the branches; one would say it was a woman, another that it was a man, until Donal himself recognized him and said:

– It is Sweeney, the king of Dal-Arie, the man that Ronan cursed on the day of the battle. That is a good man up there, he said, and if he wanted wealth and store he would be welcome to them, if only he would trust us. I am upset that Congal's people are reduced to this, for he and I had strong ties before we faced the battle. But then, Sweeney was warned by Colmcille when he went over with Congal to ask the king of Scotland for an army to field against me. Then Donal uttered the lay:

16 Sweeney, what has happened here?
Sweeney, who led hosts to war
and was the flower among them all
at Moira on that day of battle!

To see you flushed after a feast,
poppy in the gold of harvest.
Hair like shavings or like down,
your natural and perfect crown.

To see your handsome person go
was morning after a fall of snow.
The blue and crystal of your eyes
shone like deepening windswept ice.

Surefooted, elegant, except
you stumbled in the path of kingship,
you were a blooded swordsman, quick
to sense a chance and quick to strike.

Colmcille promised you, good son,
sovereignty and salvation:
how eagerly you strutted forth
blessed by that voice of heaven and earth.

Truthful seer, Colmcille
prophesied in this oracle:
All crossed the sea and here you stand
who'll never all return from Ireland.

Find the answer to his riddle
at Moira on the field of battle,
a gout of blood on a shining blade,
Congal Claon among the dead.

17 When Sweeney heard the shouts of the soldiers and
the big noise of the army, he rose out of the tree
towards the dark clouds and ranged far over mountains and territories.

A long time he went faring all through Ireland,
poking his way into hard rocky clefts,
shouldering through ivy bushes,
unsettling falls of pebbles in narrow defiles,
wading estuaries,
breasting summits,
trekking through glens,
until he found the pleasures of Glen Bolcain.

That place is a natural asylum where all the madmen
of Ireland used to assemble once their year in
madness was complete.

Glen Bolcain is like this:
it has four gaps to the wind,
pleasant woods, clean-banked wells,
cold springs and clear sandy streams
where green-topped watercress and languid
  brooklime
philander over the surface.
It is nature's pantry
with its sorrels, its wood-sorrels,
its berries, its wild garlic,
its black sloes and its brown acorns.

The madmen would beat each other for the pick of its
watercresses and for the beds on its banks.

18 Sweeney stayed a long time in that glen until one
night he was cooped up in the top of a tall ivy-grown
hawthorn. He could hardly endure it, for every time
he twisted or turned, the thorny twigs would flail him
so that he was prickled and cut and bleeding all over.
He changed from that station to another one, a clump
of thick briars with a single young blackthorn standing up out of the thorny bed, and he settled in the top
of the blackthorn. But it was too slender. It wobbled
and bent so that Sweeney fell heavily through the
thicket and ended up on the ground like a man in a
bloodbath. Then he gathered himself up, exhausted
and beaten, and came out of the thicket, saying:

– It is hard to bear this life after the pleasant times I
knew. And it has been like this a year to the night last
night!

Then he spoke this poem:

19   A year until last night
    I have lived among dark trees,
    between the flood and ebb-tide,
    going cold and naked

    with no pillow for my head,
    no human company
    and, so help me, God,
    no spear and no sword.

    No sweet talk with women.
    Instead, I pine
    for cresses, for the clean
    pickings of brooklime.

    No surge of royal blood,
    camped here in solitude;
    no glory flames the wood,
    no friends, no music.

    Tell the truth: a hard lot.
    And no shirking this fate;
    no sleep, no respite,
    no hope for a long time.

    No house, humming full,
    no men, loud with good will,
    nobody to call me king,
    no drink or banqueting.

A great gulf yawns now
between me and that retinue,
between craziness and reason.
Scavenging through the glen

on my mad royal visit:
no pomp or king's circuit
but wild scuttles in the wood.
Heavenly saints! O Holy God!

No skilled musicians' cunning,
no soft discoursing women,
no open-handed giving;
my doom to be a long dying.

Far other than tonight,
far different my plight
the times when with firm hand
I ruled over a good land.

Prospering, smiled upon,
curbing some mighty steed,
I rode high, on the full tide
of good luck and kingship.

That tide has come and gone
and spewed me up in Glen Bolcain,
disabled now, outcast
for the way I sold my Christ,

fallen almost through death's door,
drained out, spiked and torn,
under a hard-twigged bush,
the brown, jaggy hawthorn.

Our sorrows were multiplied
that Tuesday when Congal fell.
Our dead made a great harvest,
our remnant, a last swathe.

This has been my plight.
Fallen from noble heights,
grieving and astray,
a year until last night.

20 He remained in that state in Glen Bolcain until at last
he mustered his strength and flew to Cloonkill on the
borders of Bannagh and Tyrconnell. That night he
went to the edge of the well for a drink of water and a
bite of watercress and after that he went into the old
tree by the church. That was a very bad night for
Sweeney. There was a terrible storm and he des-
paired, saying:

– It is a pity I wasn't killed at Moira instead of
having to put up with hardship like this.

Then he said this poem:

21   Tonight the snow is cold.
       I was at the end of my tether
       but hunger and bother
       are endless.

       Look at me, broken
       and down-at-heel,
       Sweeney from Rasharkin.
       Look at me now,

       always shifting,
       making fresh pads,
       and always at night.
       At times I am afraid.

       In the grip of dread
       I would launch and sail
       beyond the known seas.
       I am the madman of Glen Bolcain,

       wind-scourged, stripped
       like a winter tree
       clad in black frost
       and frozen snow.

       Hard grey branches
       have torn my hands,
       the skin of my feet
       is in strips from briars

       and the pain of frostbite
       has put me astray,
       from Slemish to Slieve Gullion,
       from Slieve Gullion to Cooley.

       I went raving with grief
       on the top of Croagh Patrick,
       from Glen Bolcain to Islay,
       from Kintyre to Mourne.

I woke at dawn
with a fasting spittle:
then at Cloonkill, a bunch of cress,
then at Kilnoo, the cuckoo flower.

I wish I lived safe
and sound in Rasharkin
and not here, heartbroken,
in my bare pelt, at bay in the snow.

22 Sweeney kept going until he reached the church at
Swim-Two-Birds on the Shannon, which is now
called Cloonburren; he arrived there on a Friday, to
be exact. The clerics of the church were singing
nones, women were beating flax and one was giving
birth to a child.

– It is unseemly, said Sweeney, for the women to
violate the Lord's fast day. That woman beating the
flax reminds me of our beating at Moira.

Then he heard the vesper bell ringing and said:

– It would be sweeter to listen to the notes of the
cuckoos on the banks of the Bann than to the whinge
of this bell tonight.

Then he uttered the poem:

23   I perched for rest and imagined
cuckoos calling across water,
the Bann cuckoo, calling sweeter
than church bells that whinge and grind.

Friday is the wrong day, woman,
for you to give birth to a son,
the day when Mad Sweeney fasts
for love of God, in penitence.

Do not just discount me. Listen.
At Moira my tribe was beaten,
beetled, heckled, hammered down,
like flax being scutched by these women.

From the crag of Lough Diolar
up to Derry Colmcille
I saw great swans and heard their calls
sweetly rebuking wars and battles.

On solitary cliffs, a stag
bells and makes the whole glen shake
and re-echo. I am ravished.
Unearthly sweetness shakes my breast.

O Christ, the loving and the sinless,
hear my prayer, attend, O Christ,
and let nothing separate us.
Blend me forever in your sweetness.

24 The next day Sweeney went on to St Derville's
church, west of Erris, where he fed on watercress and
drank the water that was in the church. The night was
tempestuous, and he was shaken with grief at his
misery and deprivation. He was also homesick for
Dal-Arie and spoke these verses:

25   I pined the whole night
in Derville's chapel
for Dal-Arie
and peopled the dark

with a thousand ghosts.
My dream restored me:
the army lay at Drumfree
and I came into my kingdom,

camped with my troop,
back with Faolchu and Congal
for our night at Drumduff.
Taunters, will-o'-the-wisps,

who saw me brought to heel
at Moira, you crowd my head
and fade away
and leave me to the night.

26 Sweeney wandered Ireland for all of the next seven
years until one night he arrived back in Glen Bolcain.
That was his ark and his Eden, where he would go to
ground and would only leave when terror struck. He
stayed there that night and the next morning Lynchseachan arrived looking for him. Some say Lynchseachan was a half-brother of Sweeney's, some say he
was a foster-brother, but whichever he was, he was
deeply concerned for Sweeney and brought him back
three times out of his madness.

This time Lynchseachan was after him in the glen
and found his footprints on the bank of the stream
where Sweeney would go to eat watercress. He
also followed the trail of snapped branches where
Sweeney had shifted from tree to tree. But he did not
catch up that day, so he went into a deserted house in

the glen and lay down, fatigued by all his trailing and scouting. Soon he was in a deep sleep.

Then Sweeney, following the tracks of his tracker, was led to the house and stood listening to the snores of Lynchseachan; and consequently he came out with this poem:

27   I dare not sink down, snore and fall
fast asleep like the man at the wall,
I who never batted an eye
during the seven years since Moira.

God of Heaven! Why did I go
battling out that famous Tuesday
to end up changed into Mad Sweeney,
roosting alone up in the ivy?

From the well at Druim Crib, watercress
supplies my bit and sup at terce;
its juices that have greened my chin
are Sweeney's markings and birth-stain.

And the manhunt is an expiation.
Mad Sweeney is on the run
and sleeps curled up beneath a rag
under the shadow of Slieve League –

long cut off from the happy time
when I lived apart, an honoured name;
long exiled from those rushy hillsides,
far from my home among the reeds.

I give thanks to the King above
whose harshness only proves His love
which was outraged by my offence
and shaped my new shape for my sins –

shivering; glimpsed against the sky,
a waif alarmed out of the ivy.
Going drenched in teems of rain,
crouching under thunderstorms.

Though I still have life, haunting deep
in the yew glen, climbing mountain slopes,
I would swop places with Congal Claon,
stretched on his back among the slain.

My life is steady lamentation.
The roof above my head has gone.

I am doomed to rags, starved and mad,
brought to this by the power of God.

It was sheer madness to imagine
any life outside Glen Bolcain –
Glen Bolcain, my pillow and heart's ease,
my Eden thick with apple trees.

What does he know, the man at the wall,
how Sweeney managed since his downfall?
Going stooped through the long grass.
A sup of water. Watercress.

Summering where herons stalk.
Wintering out among wolf-packs.
Plumed with twigs that green and fall.
What does he know, the man at the wall?

I who once camped among mad friends
in Bolcain, happy glen of winds
and wind-borne echoes, live miserable
beyond the dreams of the man at the wall.

28 After that poem he arrived, on the following night, at a mill owned by Lynchseachan. The caretaker of the mill was Lynchseachan's mother-in-law, an old woman called Lonnog, daughter of Dubh Dithribh. When Sweeney went in to see her she gave him a few scraps to eat and so, for a long time, he kept coming back to the mill.

One day when Lynchseachan was out trailing him, he caught sight of Sweeney by the mill-stream, and went to speak to the old woman.

– Has Sweeney come to the mill? said Lynchseachan.

– He was here last night, said the woman.

Lynchseachan then disguised himself as his mother-in-law and sat on in the mill after she had gone, until Sweeney arrived that night. But when Sweeney saw the eyes under the shawl, he recognized Lynchseachan and at once sprang out of his reach and up through the skylight, saying:

– This is a pitiful jaunt you are on, Lynchseachan, hunting me from every place I love in Ireland. Don't you know Ronan has left me with the fears of a bird, so I cannot trust you? I am exasperated at the way you are constantly after me.

And he made this poem:

29 Lynchseachan, you are a bother.
Leave me alone, give me peace.
Is it not enough that Ronan doomed me
to live furtive and suspicious?

When I let fly that fatal spear
at Ronan in the heat of battle
it split his holy breastplate open,
it made a dent in his cleric's bell.

When I nailed him in the battle
with that magnificent spear-cast,
– Let the freedom of the birds be yours!
was how he prayed, Ronan the priest.

And I rebounded off his prayer
up, up and up, flying through air
lighter and nimbler and far higher
than I would ever fly again.

To see me in my morning glory
that Tuesday morning, turn time back:
still in my mind's eye I march out
in rank, in step with my own folk.

But now, with my own two eyes I see
a thing that's more astonishing:
under the hood of a woman's shawl,
the weather eyes of Lynchseachan.

30 – All you intend is to make me ridiculous, he said.
Leave off, harass me no more but go back to your own
place and I will go on to see Eorann.

31 When Sweeney deserted the kingship, his wife had
gone to live with Guaire. There had been two
kinsmen with equal rights to the kingship Sweeney
had abandoned, two grandsons of Scannlan's called
Guaire and Eochaidh. At that time, Eorann was with
Guaire and they had gone hunting through the Fews
towards Edenterriff in Cavan. His camp was near
Glen Bolcain, on a plain in the Armagh district.

Sweeney landed on the lintel of Eorann's hut and
spoke to her:

– Do you remember, lady, the great love we shared
when we were together? Life is still a pleasure to you
but not to me.

And this exchange ensued between them:

32 *Sweeney*:
Restless as wingbeats
of memory, I hover
above you, and your bed
still warm from your lover.

Remember when you played
the promise-game with me?
Sun and moon would have died
if ever you lost your Sweeney!

But you have broken trust,
unmade it like a bed –
not mine in the dawn frost
but yours, that he invaded.

Eorann:
Welcome here, my crazy dote,
my first and last and favourite!
I am easy now, and yet I wasted
at the cruel news of your being bested.

Sweeney:
There's more welcome for the prince
who preens for you and struts
to those amorous banquets
where Sweeney feasted once.

Eorann:
All the same, I would prefer
a hollow tree and Sweeney bare –
that sweetest game we used to play –
to banqueting with him today.

I tell you, Sweeney, if I were given
the pick of all in earth and Ireland,
I'd rather go with you, live sinless
and sup on water and watercress.

Sweeney:
But cold and hard as stone
lies Sweeney's path
through the beds of Lisardowlin.
There I go to earth

in panic, starved and bare,
a rickle of skin and bones.
I am yours no longer.
And you are another man's.

Eorann:

My poor tormented lunatic!
When I see you like this it makes me sick,
your cheek gone pale, your skin all scars,
ripped and scored by thorns and briars.

Sweeney:

And yet I hold no grudge,
my gentle one.
Christ ordained my bondage
and exhaustion.

Eorann:

I wish we could fly away together,
be rolling stones, birds of a feather:
I'd swoop to pleasure you in flight
and huddle close on the roost at night.

Sweeney:

I have gone north and south.
One night I was in the Mournes.
I have wandered as far as the Bann mouth
and Kilsooney.

33 They had no sooner finished than the army swept into the camp from every side, and as usual, he was away in panic, never stopping until twilight, when he arrived at Ros Bearaigh – that church where he first halted after the battle of Moira – and again he went into the yew tree of the church. Murtagh McEarca was erenach of the church at the time and his wife was passing the yew when by chance she caught sight of the madman. Recognizing Sweeney, she said:

– Come down out of the yew. I know you are king of Dal-Arie, and there is nobody here but myself, a woman on her own.

That is what she said, though she hoped to beguile him somehow into a trap and catch him.

– Indeed I shall not come down, said Sweeney, for Lynchseachan and his wife might come upon me. But am I not hard to recognize nowadays?

And he uttered these stanzas:

34 Only your hawk eye
could pick me out
who was cock of the walk once
in Dal-Arie –

the talk of Ireland
for style and appearance.
Since the shock of battle
I'm a ghost of myself.

So, good woman, mind
your husband and your house.
I cannot stay. But we shall meet
again on Judgement Day.

35 He cleared the tree lightly and nimbly and went on his way until he reached the old tree in Rasharkin, which was one of the three hide-outs he had in his own country, the others being at Teach mic Ninnedha and Cluan Creamha. He lodged undiscovered there for six weeks in the yew tree but he was detected in the end and the nobles of Dal-Arie held a meeting to decide who should go to apprehend him. Lynchseachan was the unanimous choice and he agreed to go.

Off he went to the tree and Sweeney was there, perched on a branch above him.

– It is a pity, Sweeney, he said, that you ended up like this, like any bird of the air, without food or drink or clothes, you that went in silk and satin and rode foreign steeds in their matchless harness. Do you remember your train, the lovely gentle women, the many young men and their hounds, the retinue of craftsmen? Do you remember the assemblies under your sway? Do you remember the cups and goblets and carved horns that flowed with pleasant heady drink? It is a pity to find you like any poor bird flitting from one waste ground to the next.

– Stop now, said Sweeney, it was my destiny. But have you any news for me about my country?

– I have indeed, said Lynchseachan, for your father is dead.

– That is a seizure, he said.

– Your mother is dead too, said the young man.

– There'll be pity from nobody now, he said.

– And your brother, said Lynchseachan.

– My side bleeds for that, said Sweeney.

– Your daughter is dead, said Lynchseachan.

– The heart's needle is an only daughter, said Sweeney.

– And your son who used to call you Daddy, said Lynchseachan.

– Indeed, he said, that is the drop that fells me to
the ground.

After that, Sweeney and Lynchseachan made up
this poem between them:

36 *Lynchseachan*:

Sweeney from the high mountains,
blooded swordsman, veteran:
for the sake of Christ, your judge and saviour,
speak to me, your foster-brother.

If you hear me, listen. Listen,
my royal lord, my great prince,
for I bring, as gently as I can,
the bad news from your native ground.

You left behind a dead kingdom
and that is why I had to come
with tidings of a dead brother,
a father dead, a dead mother.

Sweeney:

If my gentle mother's dead, I face
a harder exile from my place;
yet she had cooled in love of me
and love that's cooled is worse than pity.

The son whose father's lately dead
kicks the trace and lives unbridled.
His pain's a branch bowed down with nuts.
A dead brother is a wounded side.

Lynchseachan:

Things that the world already knows
I still must break to you as news:
thin as you are, and starved, your wife
pined after you, and died of grief.

Sweeney:

A household when the wife is gone,
a boat that's rudderless in storm;
it is pens of feathers next the skin;
a widower at his bleak kindling.

Lynchseachan:

Sorrow accumulates: heartbreak,
keens and wailings fill the air.
But all of that's like a fist round smoke
now that you have lost your sister.

Sweeney:

No common wisdom I might invoke
can stanch the wound from such a stroke.
A sister's love is still, unselfish,
like sunlight mild upon a ditch.

Lynchseachan:

Our north is colder than it was,
calves are kept in from their cows
since your daughter and sister's son,
who both loved you, were stricken down.

Sweeney:

My faithful hound, my faithful nephew –
no bribe could buy their love of me.
But you've unstitched the rent of sorrow.
The heart's needle is an only daughter.

Lynchseachan:

I have to tell what I would keep back.
It wounds me to the very quick!
In Dal-Arie, everyone
laments the death of your son.

Sweeney:

This is the news that daunts all men.
This is the thing that brings us down –
the loss, the wound in memory,
the death of him who called me *Daddy*.

This is a blow I cannot stand.
Here my resistance has to end.
You are the beater, I the bird
frightened and driven out of covert.

Lynchseachan:

Sweeney, now you are in my hands,
I tell you I can heal these wounds.
None of your family's in the grave.
All your people are alive.

Calm yourself. Come to. Rest.
Come home east. Forget the west.
Admit, Sweeney, you have come too far
from where your heart's affections are.

Woods and forests and wild deer –
things like these delight you more
than sleeping in your eastern dun
on a bed of feather-down.

Near a quick mill-pond, your perch
on a dark green holly branch
means far more now than any feast
among the brightest and the best.

Harp music in the breasting hills
would not soothe you: you would still
strain to hear from the oak-wood
the brown stag belling to the herd.

Swifter than the wind in glens,
once the figure of a champion,
now a legend, and a madman –
your exile's over, Sweeney. Come.

37 When Sweeney heard the news of his only son he fell
from the yew tree and Lynchseachan caught him and
put manacles on him. Then he told him that all his
people were alive, and escorted him back to the
assembled nobles of Dal-Arie. They produced locks
and fetters in which they shackled Sweeney and left
him under Lynchseachan's supervision for the next
six weeks. During that time the nobles of the province
kept visiting him, and at the end of it, his sense and
memory came back to him and he felt himself
restored to his old shape and manner. So they took
the tackle off him and he was back to his former self,
the man they had known as king.

After that, Sweeney was quartered in Lynchseachan's bedroom. Then harvest time came round
and one day Lynchseachan went with his people to
reap. Sweeney, shut in the bedroom, was left in the
care of the mill-hag, who was warned not to speak to
him. All the same, she did speak to him, asking him to
relate some of his adventures when he was in his state
of madness.

– A curse on your mouth, hag, said Sweeney, for
your talk is dangerous. God will not allow me to go
mad again.

– It was your insult to Ronan that put you mad, said
the hag.

– This is hateful, he said, to have to put up with
your treachery and trickery.

– It is no treachery, only the truth.

And Sweeney said:

38 *Sweeney*:

Hag, did you come here from your mill
to spring me over wood and hill?
Is it to be a woman's ploy
and treachery send me astray?

The Hag:

Sweeney, your sorrows are well known,
but I am not the treacherous one:
the miracles of holy Ronan
maddened and drove you among madmen.

Sweeney:

If I were king and I wish I were
again the king who held sway here,
instead of the banquet and ale-mug
I'd give you a fist on the mouth, hag.

39 – Now listen, woman, he said, if you only knew the
hard times I have been through. Many's the dreadful
leap I have leaped from hill and fort and land and
valley.

– For God's sake, said the hag, let me see one of
those leaps now. Show me how you did it when you
were off in your madness.

With that, he bounded over the bed-rail and lit on
the end of the bench.

– Sure I could do that leap myself, said the hag,
and she did it.

Then Sweeney took another leap out through the
skylight of the lodge.

– I could do that too, said the hag, and leaped it,
there and then.

Anyhow, this is the way it ended up: Sweeney went
lifting over five cantreds of Dal-Arie that day until he
arrived at Gleann na n-Eachtach in Feegile and she
was on his heels the whole way. When he took a rest
there, in the top of an ivy-bunch, the hag perched on
another tree beside him.

It was the end of the harvest season and Sweeney
heard a hunting-call from a company in the skirts of
the wood.

– This will be the outcry of the Ui Faolain coming
to kill me, he said. I slew their king at Moira and this
host is out to avenge him.

He heard the stag bellowing and he made a poem
in which he praised aloud all the trees of Ireland, and

rehearsed some of his own hardships and sorrows,
saying:

40   Suddenly this bleating
and belling in the glen!
The little timorous stag
like a scared musician

startles my heartstrings
with high homesick refrains –
deer on my lost mountains,
flocks out on the plain.

The bushy leafy oak tree
is highest in the wood,
the forking shoots of hazel
hide sweet hazel-nuts.

The alder is my darling,
all thornless in the gap,
some milk of human kindness
coursing in its sap.

The blackthorn is a jaggy creel
stippled with dark sloes;
green watercress in thatch on wells
where the drinking blackbird goes.

Sweetest of the leafy stalks,
the vetches strew the pathway;
the oyster-grass is my delight,
and the wild strawberry.

Low-set clumps of apple trees
drum down fruit when shaken;
scarlet berries clot like blood
on mountain rowan.

Briars curl in sideways,
arch a stickle back,
draw blood and curl up innocent
to sneak the next attack.

The yew tree in each churchyard
wraps night in its dark hood.
Ivy is a shadowy
genius of the wood.

Holly rears its windbreak,
a door in winter's face;

life-blood on a spear-shaft
darkens the grain of ash.

Birch tree, smooth and blessed,
delicious to the breeze,
high twigs plait and crown it
the queen of trees.

The aspen pales
and whispers, hesitates:
a thousand frightened scuts
race in its leaves.

But what disturbs me most
in the leafy wood
is the to and fro and to and fro
of an oak rod.

Ronan was dishonoured,
he rang his cleric's bell:
my spasm and outrage
brought curse and miracle.

And noble Congal's armour,
his tunic edged in gold,
swathed me in doomed glory
with omens in each fold.

His lovely tunic marked me
in the middle of the rout,
the host pursuing, shouting:
– The one in the gold coat.

Get him, take him live or dead,
every man fall to.
Draw and quarter, pike
and spit him, none will blame you.

Still the horsemen followed
across the north of Down,
my back escaping nimbly
from every javelin thrown.

As if I had been cast
by a spearsman, I flew high,
my course a whisper in the air,
a breeze flicking through ivy.

I overtook the startled fawn,
kept step with his fleet step,

I caught, I rode him lightly –
from peak to peak we leapt,

mountain after mountain,
a high demented spree
from Inishowen south,
and south, as far as Galtee.

From Galtee up to Liffey
I was swept along and driven
on through bitter twilight
to the slopes of Benn Bulben.

And that was the first night
of my long restless vigil:
my last night at rest,
the eve of Congal's battle.

And then Glen Bolcain was my lair,
my earth and den;
I've scaled and strained against those slopes
by star and moon.

I wouldn't swop a lonely hut
in that dear glen
for a world of moorland acres
on a russet mountain.

Its water flashing like wet grass,
its wind so keen,
its tall brooklime, its watercress
the greenest green.

I love the ancient ivy tree,
the pale-leafed sallow,
the birch's sibilant melody,
the solemn yew.

And you, Lynchseachan, can try
disguise, deceit;
come in the mask and shawl of night,
I won't be caught.

You managed it the first time
with your litany of the dead:
father, mother, daughter, son,
brother, wife – you lied

but if you want your say again,
then be ready

to face the heights and crags of Mourne
to follow me.

I would live happy
in an ivy bush
high in some twisted tree
and never come out.

The skylarks rising
into their high space
send me pitching and tripping
over stumps on the moor

and my hurry flushes
the turtle-dove.
I overtake it,
my plumage rushing,

am startled then
by the startled woodcock
or a blackbird's sudden
volubility.

Think of my alarms,
my coming to earth
where the fox still
gnaws at the bones,

my wild career
as the wolf from the wood
goes tearing ahead
and I lift towards the mountain,

the bark of foxes
echoing below me,
the wolves behind me
howling and rending –

their vapoury tongues
their low-slung speed
shaken off like nightmare
at the foot of the slope.

If I show my heels
I am hobbled by guilt.
I am a sheep
without a fold

who sleeps his sound sleep
in the old tree at Kilnoo,

dreaming back the good days
with Congal in Antrim.

A starry frost will come
dropping on the pools
and I'll be out
on unsheltered hills:

herons calling
in cold Glenelly,
flocks of birds quickly
coming and going.

I prefer the scurry
and song of blackbirds
to the usual blather
of men and women.

I prefer the squeal of badgers
in their sett
to the hullabuloo
of the morning hunt.

I prefer the re-
echoing belling of a stag
among the peaks
to that terrible horn.

Those unharnessed runners
from glen to glen!
Nobody tames
that royal blood,

each one aloof
on its rightful summit,
antlered, watchful.
Imagine them,

the stag of high Slieve Felim,
the stag of the steep Fews,
the stag of Duhallow, the stag of Orrery,
the fierce stag of Killarney.

The stag of Islandmagee, Larne's stag,
the stag of Moylinny,
the stag of Cooley, the stag of Cunghill,
the stag of the two-peaked Burren.

The mother of this herd
is old and grey,

the stags that follow her
are branchy, many-tined.

I would be cloaked in the grey
sanctuary of her head,
I would roost among
her mazy antlers

and would be lofted into
this thicket of horns
on the stag that lows at me
over the glen.

I am Sweeney, the whinger,
the scuttler in the valley.
But call me, instead,
Peak-pate, Stag-head.

The springs I always liked
were the fountain at Dunmall
and the spring-well on Knocklayde
that tasted pure and cool.

Forever mendicant,
my rags all frayed and scanty,
high in the mountains
like a crazed, frost-bitten sentry

I find no bed nor quarter,
no easy place in the sun –
not even in this reddening
covert of tall fern.

My only rest: eternal
sleep in holy ground
when Moling's earth lets fall
its dark balm on my wound.

But now that sudden bleating
and belling in the glen!
I am a timorous stag
feathered by Ronan Finn.

41 After that poem, Sweeney went on from Feegile
through Bannagh, Benevenagh and Maghera but he
could not shake off the hag until he reached Dunseverick in Ulster. There he leaped from the summit of
the fort, down a sheer drop, coaxing the hag to follow.
She leaped quickly after him but fell on the cliff of
Dunseverick, where she was smashed to pieces and

scattered into the sea. That is how she got her end on Sweeney's trail.

42 Then Sweeney said:

– From now on, I won't tarry in Dal-Arie because Lynchseachan would have my life to avenge the hag's.

So he proceeded to Roscommon in Connacht, where he alighted on the bank of the well and treated himself to watercress and water. But when a woman came out of the erenach's house, he panicked and fled, and she gathered the watercress from the stream. Sweeney watched her from his tree and greatly lamented the theft of his patch of cress, saying:

– It is a shame that you are taking my watercress. If only you knew my plight, how I am unpitied by tribesman or kinsman, how I am no longer a guest in any house on the ridge of the world. Watercress is my wealth, water is my wine, and hard bare trees and soft tree bowers are my friends. Even if you left that cress, you would not be left wanting; but if you take it, you are taking the bite from my mouth.

And he made this poem:

43 Woman, picking the watercress
and scooping up my drink of water,
were you to leave them as my due
you would still be none the poorer.

Woman, have consideration!
We two go two different ways:
I perch out among tree-tops,
you lodge here in a friendly house.

Woman, have consideration.
Think of me in the sharp wind,
forgotten, past consideration,
without a cloak to wrap me in.

Woman, you cannot start to know
sorrows Sweeney has forgotten:
how friends were so long denied him
he killed his gift for friendship even.

Fugitive, deserted, mocked
by memories of my days as king,
no longer called to head the troop
when warriors are mustering,

no longer the guest of honour
at tables anywhere in Ireland,
ranging like a mad pilgrim
over rock-peaks on the mountain.

The harper who harped me to rest,
where is his soothing music now?
My people too, my kith and kin,
where did their affection go?

In my heyday, on horseback,
I rode high into my own:
now memory's an unbroken horse
that rears and suddenly throws me down.

Over starlit moors and plains,
woman taking my watercress,
to his cold and lonely station
the shadow of that Sweeney goes

with watercresses for his herds
and cold water for his mead,
bushes for companions,
the naked hillside for his bed.

Hugging these, my cold comforts,
ever hungering after cress,
above the bare plain of Emly
I hear cries of the wild geese,

and still bowed to my hard yoke,
still a bag of skin and bone,
I reel as if a blow hit me
and fly off at the cry of a heron

to land in Dairbre, maybe,
in spring, when days are on the turn,
to scare away again by twilight
westward, into the Mournes.

Gazing down at clean gravel,
to lean out over a cool well,
drink a mouthful of sunlit water
and gather cress by the handful –

even this you would pluck from me,
lean pickings that have thinned my blood
and chilled me on the cold uplands,
hunkering low when winds spring up.

Morning wind is the coldest wind,
it flays me of my rags, it freezes –
the very memory leaves me speechless,
woman, picking the watercress.

Woman:
Sweeney, be merciful to me.
Leave retribution to the Lord.
Judge not and you won't be judged.
Triumph and bless. Do not be hard.

Sweeney:
Then here is justice, fair and even,
from my high court in the yew:
if you leave the cress for me,
I shall leave my rags in lieu.

I have no place to lay my head.
Human love has failed me. So
let me swop my sins for cress,
let me make a scapegoat of you.

Your greed has left me hungering.
Therefore, may all you robbed me of
come between you and good luck
and leave you hungering for love.

As you snatched cress, may you be snatched
by the foraging, blue-coated Norse.
And live eaten by remorse.
And cursing God that our paths crossed.

44 He stayed in Roscommon that night and the next day
he went on to Slieve Aughty, from there to the
pleasant slopes of Slemish, then on to the high peaks
of Slieve Bloom, and from there to Inishmurray. After
that, he stayed six weeks in a cave that belonged to
Donnan on the island of Eig off the west of Scotland.
From there he went on to Ailsa Craig, where he spent
another six weeks, and when he finally left there he
bade the place farewell and bewailed his state, like
this:

45   Without bed or board
        I face dark days
        in frozen lairs
        and wind-driven snow.

Ice scoured by winds.
Watery shadows from weak sun.
Shelter from the one tree
on a plateau.

Haunting deerpaths,
enduring rain,
first-footing the grey
frosted grass.

I climb towards the pass
and the stag's belling
rings off the wood,
surf-noise rises

where I go, heartbroken
and worn out,
sharp-haunched Sweeney,
raving and moaning.

The sough of the winter night,
my feet packing the hailstones
as I pad the dappled
banks of Mourne

or lie, unslept, in a wet bed
on the hills by Lough Erne,
tensed for first light
and an early start.

Skimming the waves
at Dunseverick,
listening to billows
at Dun Rodairce,

hurtling from that great wave
to the wave running
in tidal Barrow,
one night in hard Dun Cernan,

the next among the wild flowers
of Benn Boirne;
and then a stone pillow
on the screes of Croagh Patrick.

I shift restlessly
on the plain of Boroma,
from Benn Iughoine
to Benn Boghaine.

Then that woman
interfered,
disturbed me
and affronted me

and made off with
the bite from my mouth.
It is retribution
and it is constant.

I gather cress
in delicious bunches,
four round handfuls
in Glen Bolcain,

and then I unpick
the shy bog-berry,
then drink water
from Ronan's well.

My nails are bent,
my loins weak,
my feet bleeding,
my thighs bare –

and I'll be overtaken
by a stubborn band
of Ulstermen
faring through Scotland.

But to have ended up
lamenting here
on Ailsa Craig.
A hard station!

Ailsa Craig,
the seagulls' home,
God knows it is
hard lodgings.

Ailsa Craig,
bell-shaped rock,
reaching sky-high,
snout in the sea –

it hard-beaked,
me seasoned and scraggy:
we mated like a couple
of hard-shanked cranes.

I tread the slop
and foam of beds,
unlooked for,
penitential,

and imagine treelines
far away
a banked-up, soothing
wooded haze,

not like the swung
depths and swells
of that nightmare-black
lough in Mourne.

I need woods
for consolation,
some grove in Meath –
or the space of Ossory.

Or Ulster in harvest.
Strangford, shimmering.
Or a summer visit
to green Tyrone.

At Lammas I migrate
to the pools of Teltown,
pass the springtime fishing
bends of the Shannon.

I often get as far
as my old domain,
those groomed armies,
those stern hillsides.

46 Then Sweeney left Ailsa Craig and flew over the
stormy maw of the sea to the land of the Britons. He
passed their royal stronghold on his right and dis-
covered a great wood where he could hear wailing and
lamentation. Sometimes it was a great moan of
anguish, sometimes an exhausted sigh. The moaner
turned out to be another madman astray in the wood.
Sweeney approached him.

– Who are you, friend? Sweeney asked.

– A madman, said he.

– In that case, you are a friend indeed. I am a
madman myself, said Sweeney. Why don't you join up
with me?

– I would, the other man said, except that I am in

dread of the king or the king's retinue capturing me, and I am not sure that you are not one of them.

– I am no such thing, said Sweeney, and since you can trust me, tell me your name.

– They call me the Man of the Wood, said the madman.

Then Sweeney spoke this verse and the Man of the Wood answered as follows:

47 *Sweeney*:

What happened, Man of the Wood,
to make you whinge
and hobble like this? Why did
your mind unhinge?

Man:

Caution and fear of the king
have silenced me.
I made a tombstone of my tongue
to keep my story.

I am the Man of the Wood.
I was famous
in battles once. Now I hide
among bushes.

Sweeney:

I come from the Bush myself.
I am Sweeney,
son of Colman. Like yourself,
outcast, shifty.

48 After that, they did confide in each other and shared their life stories. Sweeney said to the madman:

– Tell me about yourself.

– I am a landowner's son, said the mad Briton, a native of this country, and my name is Alan.

– Tell me, Sweeney asked, what made you mad?

– It is simple. Once upon a time there were two kings in this country, struggling for the kingship. Their names were Eochaidh and Cuagu. Eochaidh was the better king and I am one of his people. Anyhow, the issue was to be decided at a great muster where there was to be a battle. I laid solemn obligations on each of my chief's people that none was to come to the battle unless he was arrayed in silk. I did this so that they would be magnificent, outstanding beyond the others in pomp and panoply. But, for

doing that, the hosts cursed me with three howls of malediction that sent me astray and frightened, the way you see me.

49 In the same way he asked Sweeney what drove him to madness.

– The words of Ronan, said Sweeney. At the battle of Moira he cursed me in front of the armies so that I sprang out of the battle and have been wandering and fleeing ever since.

– O Sweeney, said Alan, since we have trusted each other, let us now be guardians to each other.

Whoever of us is the first to hear
the cry of a heron from a lough's blue-green waters
or the clear note of a cormorant
or the flight of a woodcock off a branch
or the wheep of a plover disturbed in its sleep
or the crackle of feet in withered branches,
or whoever of us is the first to see
the shadow of a bird above the wood,
let him warn the other.
Let us move always
with the breadth of two trees between us.
And if one of us hears any of these things
or anything like them,
let both of us scatter immediately.

50 So they went about like that for a year. At the end of the year Alan said to Sweeney:

– Today is the day we must part, for the end of my life has come, and I will go where I am destined to meet my death.

– How will you die? Sweeney asked.

– That is simple, Alan said. I will proceed now to the waterfall at Doovey, where a blast of wind will unbalance me and pitch me into the waterfall, so that I'll be drowned. Afterwards, I will be buried in the churchyard of a saint. And I'll go to heaven. And now, Sweeney, said Alan, tell me what your own fate will be.

Sweeney told him what this story goes on to tell and they parted. The Briton set out for the waterfall and when he reached it he was drowned in it.

51 Then Sweeney came to Ireland, reaching the plain of Moylinny, in Antrim, as the evening was drawing on. When he realized where he was, he said:

– This was always a good plain, and I was here once with a good man. That was Scannlan's son, my friend Congal Claon. One day here I said to Congal that I wanted to go to another lord and master because the rewards I got from him were too small. To persuade me to stay with him, Congal immediately gave me a hundred and fifty lovely horses, and his own brown steed into the bargain; and a hundred and fifty flashing swords, hafted in tusks; fifty servants and fifty servant girls; a tunic made of cloth-of-gold, and a magnificent girdle of chequered silk.

Then Sweeney recited this poem:

52 Now my bare skin feels
night falling on Moylinny,
the plain where Congal lived.
Now in my memory

I see Congal and me
riding across the plain
deep in conversation,
headed for Drum Lurgan.

I am saying to the king:
– The services I give
are not being rewarded.
And I threaten I will leave.

What does the king do then?
He gives me in their hundreds
horses, bridles, swords, foreign
captives, girl attendants.

And my great chestnut steed,
the best that grazed or galloped,
his cloth-of-gold tunic,
his girdle of silk plaits.

So what plain matches this plain?
Is it the plain of Meath
or the plain of Airgeadros
or Moyfevin with its crosses?

Moylurg or Moyfea,
the lovely plain of Connacht,
the Liffey banks, Bannside,
or the plain of Muirhevna?

I have seen all of them,
north, south, east, and west,
but never saw the equal
of this ground in Antrim.

53 When he had made that poem Sweeney came on to Glen Bolcain, where he went wandering freely until he met with a madwoman. He shied and ran away from her, yet divining somehow that she too was simple-minded, he stopped in his tracks and turned to her. With that, she shied and ran away from him.

– Alas, God, Sweeney said, life is a misery. I scare away from her and she scares away from me. And in Glen Bolcain, of all places!

Then he began:

54 Whoever stirs up enmity
should never have been born;
may every bitter man and woman
be barred at the gate of heaven.

If three conspire and combine,
one will backbite or complain
as I complain, going torn
by briar and sharp blackthorn.

First, madwoman flees from man.
Then, it's something stranger even:
barefoot, in his bare skin,
the man is running from the woman.

In November, wild ducks fly.
From those dark evenings until May
let us forage, nest and hide
in ivy in the brown-floored wood

and hear behind the late birds' song
sounds of water in Glen Bolcain,
its streams, all hurry, hush and jabber,
its islands in the forking rivers,

its hazel trees and holly bowers,
its leaves, its acorns and its briars,
its nuts, its sharp-tasting sloes,
all its cool-fleshed winter-berries:

and under trees, its hounds coursing,
its dappled antlered stags belling,
its water's endless, endless fall –
sounds of water in Glen Bolcain.

55 After that, Sweeney went to the house where his wife, Eorann, was lodging with her retinue of maid-servants. He stood at the outer door of the house and spoke to his former queen:

– Here you are, Eorann, laid in the lap of luxury, and still there is no lap for me to lie in.

– That is how it is, Eorann said, but come in.

– Indeed I will not, said Sweeney, in case the army traps me in the house.

– Well, said the woman, it seems your mind has not got any better, and since you do not want to stop with us, why don't you go away and leave us in peace? There are people here who knew you when you were in your right mind; it would be an embarrassment if they were to see you like this.

– Isn't that terrible? said Sweeney. Now I know it. It is fatal to trust a woman. And I was generous to this one. She is spurning me now but I would have been the man of the moment if I had come back that day when I slew Oilill Caedach, the king of Ui Faolain.

And with that he said:

56   Any man a woman falls for,
       however handsome, should beware.
       Sweeney is the living proof,
       he was cast off by his love.

       And any trusting man must stay
       on guard against their treachery:
       betrayal such as mine by Eorann
       is second nature in a woman.

       Gullible, open-handed,
       straightforward and wide-eyed,
       I gave my steeds and herds away,
       filled her pastures in a day.

       In the thick of fighting men
       I could more than hold my own:
       when the battle cry was sounded
       I handled thirty single-handed.

       It was Congal's right to ask for
       a warrior to champion Ulster:
       – Who among you will take on
       the fighter king of Ui Faolain?

       Oilill was a berserk giant,
       a shield and spear in either hand,
       so overbearing in his stride
       for a while our ranks were daunted.

       But when I spoke at Congal's side
       it was not to whinge or backslide:
       – Though Oilill is their strongest bastion,
       I will hold the line against him.

       I left him shortened by a head
       and left the torso, overjoyed,
       and left five other princes dead
       before I stopped to wipe my blade.

57 With that, Sweeney rose lightly and stealthily and went hopping airily from peak to peak, from one hill to the next, until he reached Mourne in the south of Ulster. He rested there, saying:

– This is a good place for a madman, but it is no place for corn or milk or food. And though it is a lovely, lofty station, it is still uncomfortable and uneasy. There is no shelter here from the storm or the shower.

And then he uttered these words:

58   The Mournes are cold tonight,
       my quarters are desolate:
       no milk or honey in this land
       of drifted snow and gusting wind.

       And my bed is cold at night
       up here on the naked summit.
       In a sharp-branched holly tree
       I cower and shiver and waste away.

       The pools are ice, frost hardens on me.
       I shake myself and then break free,
       coming alive like a fanned ember
       in stormwinds sweeping north from Leinster,

       and dreaming, when the summer dies
       round Hallowe'en and All Hallows,
       of another move to my old ground –
       the clear well-waters of Glen Bolcain.

       Astray no more then east or west,
       blizzards whipping my bare face,
       not shivering in some drifted den,
       a starved, pinched, raving madman,

but sheltered in that lovely arbour,
my winter haven and my harbour,
my refuge from the bare heath,
my royal fort, my king's rath.

Every night I glean and raid
and comb the floor of the oak wood.
My hands work into leaf and rind,
old roots, old windfalls on the ground,

they rake through matted watercress
and grope among the bog-berries,
cool brooklime, sorrel and damp moss,
wild garlic and wild raspberries,

apples, hazel-nuts and acorns,
the haws of sharp, jaggy hawthorns,
the blackberries, the floating weed,
the whole store of the oak wood.

Keep me here, Christ, far away
from open ground and flat country.
Let me suffer the cold of glens.
I dread the cold space of the plains.

59 The next morning Sweeney started again. He passed
Moyfevin and the clear, green-wavering Shannon; he
passed the inviting slopes of Aughty, the spreading
pastures of Loughrea, the delightful banks of the
River Suck, and landed on the shores of broad Lough
Ree. He spent that night in the fork of Bile Tiobradain, which was one of his favourite hide-outs in the
country. It was Creegaille, in the east of Connacht.

Great sorrow and misery descended on him and he
said:

– Indeed I have suffered great trouble and distress.
It was cold in the Mournes last night and it is no
better tonight in the fork of Bile Tiobradain.

60 It was snowing that night, and as fast as the snow fell,
it was frozen. So he said:

– I have endured purgatories since the feathers
grew on me. And still there is no respite. I realize, he
said, that even if it were to mean my death, it would be
better to trust my people than to endure these woes
forever.

Then he recited the poem, proclaiming aloud his
woes:

61 Almighty God, I deserved this,
my cut feet, my drained face,
winnowed by a sheer wind
and miserable in my mind.

Last night I lay in Mourne
plastered in wet; cold rain poured.
Tonight, in torment, in Glasgally
I am crucified in the fork of a tree.

I who endured unflinchingly
through long nights and long days
since the feathers penned my frame
foresee nothing but the same.

Hard weather has withered me,
blizzards have buried me.
As I wince here in cutting wind
Glen Bolcain's heather haunts my mind.

Unsettled, panicky, astray,
I course over the whole country
from River Liffey to Lower Bann,
from Bannside to the banks of Lagan;

then over Rathmore to Roscommon,
and fields that lie around Cruachan,
above Moylurg's level plain
and the brow of bushy Fews Mountain.

Or else I make a tough migration
to the Knockmealdown mountains;
or from Glasgally, a long glide
eastward to a Louth hillside.

All this is hard to thole, Lord!
Still without bed or board,
crouching to graze on cress,
drinking cold water from rivers.

Alarmed out of the autumn wood,
whipped by whins, flecked with blood,
running wild among wolf-packs,
shying away with the red stag.

Son of God, have mercy on us!
Never to hear a human voice!
To sleep naked every night
up there in the highest thickets,

to have lost my proper shape and looks,
a mad scuttler on mountain peaks,
a derelict doomed to loneliness:
Son of God, have mercy on us!

62 – All the same, Sweeney said, even if Donal, son of
Aodh, were to kill me, I will still go to Dal-Arie and
trust to the mercy of my own people. If the mill-hag
had not duped me into that bout of leaping, I would
still be sane enough.

63 Then a glimmer of reason came back to him and he
set out for his own country, ready to settle there and
entrust himself to the people.

Ronan heard of Sweeney's return to his senses and
his decision to go back among his own, and cried out:
– I beseech you, Lord, that the persecutor may not
come near the church to torment it again; I beseech
you, do not relent in your vengeance or ease his
affliction until he is sundered body from soul in his
death-swoon. Remember that you struck him for an
example, a warning to tyrants that you and your
people were sacred and not to be lightly dishonoured
or outraged.

64 God answered Ronan's prayer. When Sweeney was
out on the uplands of the Fews he halted, stalk still: a
strange apparition rose before him at midnight.
Bleeding headless torsos and disembodied heads –
five scraggy, goat-bearded heads – screamed and
bounced this way and that over the road. When he got
among them, they were talking to each other.
– He is a madman, said the first head.
– A madman from Ulster, said the second.
– Follow him well, said the third.
– May the pursuit be long, said the fourth.
– Until he reaches the sea, said the fifth.
They rose in a flock, coming for him, but he soared
away in front, skimming from thicket to thicket; and
no matter how wide the glen that opened before him,
he bounded from edge to edge, from the top of one
hill to the top of the next.

65 The heads were pursuing him,
lolling and baying,
snapping and yelping,
whining and squealing.

They nosed at his calves and his thighs,
they breathed on his shoulder,
they nuzzled the back of his neck,
they went bumping off tree-trunks and rock-face,
they spouted and plunged like a waterfall,
until he gave them the slip and escaped
in a swirling tongue of low cloud.

66 He had lost them, goat-head and dog-head and the
whole terrifying pack he had sensed there. But his
previous wandering and flying were nothing com-
pared with what he suffered now, for he was startled
into a fit which lasted six weeks until he perched one
night in the top of a tree, on the summit of Slieve
Eidhneach. In the morning he began lamenting:

67 My dark night has come round again.
The world goes on but I return
to haunt myself. I freeze and burn.
I am the bare figure of pain.

Frost crystals and the level ice,
the scourging snow, the male-voiced storm,
they all perform my requiem.
My hearth goes cold, my fire dies.

Are there still some who call me prince?
The King of Kings, the Lord of All
revoked my title, worked my downfall,
unhoused, unwived me for my sins.

Why did He spare my life at Moira?
Why did He grudge me death in battle?
Why ordained the hag of the mill
His hound of heaven and my fury?

The mill-hag's millstone round my neck!
Hell roast her soul! She dragged me down
when I leaped up in agitation.
I fell for that old witch's trick.

Then Lynchseachan was in full cry,
a bloodhound never off my trail.
I fell for his lies too and fell
among captors out of the tree.

They made me face the love I'd lost.
They tied me up and carried me
back to the house. The mockery!
I overheard their victory feast

yet gradually grew self-possessed,
for there were decent people there,
and gaming and constant laughter.
My mind was knitting up at last

but soon unravelled into nightmare.
I was for the high jump once more.
The mill-hag spun her web and swore
her innocence. I leaped for her

and leaped beyond the bounds of sense.
She challenged me a second time.
We kept in step like words in rhyme.
I set the pace and led the dance –

I cleared the skylight and the roof,
I flew away beyond the fortress
but she hung on. Through smooth and rough
I raised the wind and led the chase.

We coursed all over Ireland then.
I was the wind and she was smoke.
I was the prow and she the wake.
I was the earth and she the moon.

But always look before you leap!
Though she was fit for bog and hill,
Dunseverick gave her the spill.
She followed me down off the top

of the fort and spread-eagled
her bitch's body in the air.
I trod the water, watching her
hit the rocks. And I was glad

to see her float in smithereens.
A crew of devils made a corpse
of her and buried it. Cursed
be the ground that housed her bones.

One night I walked across the Fews –
the hills were dark, the starlight dead –
when suddenly five severed heads,
five lantern ghouls, appeared and rose

like bats from hell, surrounding me.
Then a head spoke – another shock!
– This is the Ulster lunatic.
Let us drive him into the sea!

I went like an arrow from a bow.
My feet disdained that upland ground.
Goat-head and dog-head cursed but found
me impossible to follow.

I have deserved all this:
night-vigils, terror,
flittings across water,
women's cried-out eyes.

68 One time during his wild career Sweeney left Slieve
Lougher and landed in Feegile. He stayed there for a
year among the clear streams and branches of the
wood, eating red holly-berries and dark brown
acorns, and drinking from the River Feegile. At the
end of that time, deep grief and sorrow settled over
him because of his terrible life; so he came out with
this short poem:

69   Look at Sweeney now, alas!
        His body mortified and numb,
        unconsoled, sleepless
        in the rough blast of the storm.

        From Slieve Lougher I came
        to the border marches of Feegile,
        my diet still the usual
        ivy-berries and oak-mast.

        I spent a whole year on the mountain
        enduring my transformation,
        dabbing, dabbing like a bird
        at the holly-berry's crimson.

        My grief is raw and constant.
        Tonight all my strength is gone.
        Who has more cause to lament
        than Mad Sweeney of Glen Bolcain?

70 One day Sweeney went to Drum Iarann in Connacht
where he stole some watercress and drank from a
green-flecked well. A cleric came out of the church,
full of indignation and resentment, calling Sweeney a
well-fed, contented madman, and reproaching him
where he cowered in the yew tree:

71 *Cleric*:
        Aren't you the contented one?
        You eat my watercress,

then you perch in the yew tree
beside my little house.

Sweeney:
  Contented's not the word!
  I am so terrified,
  so panicky, so haunted
  I dare not bat an eyelid.

  The flight of a small wren
  scares me as much, bell-man,
  as a great expedition
  out to hunt me down.

  Were you in my place, monk,
  and I in yours, think:
  would you enjoy being mad?
  Would you be contented?

72 Once when Sweeney was rambling and raking
through Connacht he ended up in Alternan in
Tireragh. A community of holy people had made
their home there, and it was a lovely valley, with a
turbulent river shooting down the cliff; trees fruited
and blossomed on the cliff-face; there were shelter-
ing ivies and heavy-topped orchards, there were wild
deer and hares and fat swine; and sleek seals, that
used to sleep on the cliff, having come in from the
ocean beyond. Sweeney coveted the place mightily
and sang its praises aloud in this poem:

73   Sainted cliff at Alternan,
      nut grove, hazel-wood!
      Cold quick sweeps of water
      fall down the cliff-side.

      Ivies green and thicken there,
      its oak-mast is precious.
      Fruited branches nod and bend
      from heavy-headed apple trees.

      Badgers make their setts there
      and swift hares have their form;
      and seals' heads swim the ocean,
      cobbling the running foam.

      And by the waterfall, Colman's son,
      Ronan of Drumgesh's victim,
      haggard, spent, frost-bitten Sweeney,
      is sleeping at the foot of a tree.

74 At last Sweeney arrived where Moling lived, the place
that is known as St Mullins. Just then, Moling was
addressing himself to Kevin's psalter and reading
from it to his students. Sweeney presented himself at
the brink of the well and began to eat watercress.
  – Aren't you the early bird? said the cleric; and
continued, with Sweeney answering, as follows:

75 *Moling*:
  So, you would steal a march on us,
  up and breakfasting so early!
Sweeney:
  Not so very early, priest.
  Terce has come in Rome already.

Moling:
  And what knowledge has a fool
  about the hour of terce in Rome?
Sweeney:
  The Lord makes me His oracle
  from sunrise till sun's going down.

Moling:
  Then speak to us of hidden things,
  give us tidings of the Lord.
Sweeney:
  Not I. But if you are Moling,
  you are gifted with the Word.

Moling:
  Mad as you are, you are sharp-witted.
  How do you know my face and name?
Sweeney:
  In my days astray I rested
  in this enclosure many a time.

Moling:
  But Sweeney, son of Colman Cuar,
  why won't you settle in one place?
Sweeney:
  The resting place that I prefer
  is life in everlasting peace.

Moling:
  God help you then. Do you not dread
  the slippery brim of hell's wide mouth?
Sweeney:
  My one affliction is that God
  denies me all repose on earth.

Moling:

    Come closer then. Come here and share
    whatever morsels you would like.

Sweeney:

    There are worse things, priest, than hunger.
    Imagine living without a cloak.

Moling:

    Then you are welcome to my smock,
    welcome to my cowl as well.

Sweeney:

    Sometimes memory brings back
    times it hurts me to recall.

Moling:

    Are you Sweeney, the bogey-man,
    escaped out of the fight at Moira?

Sweeney:

    I am the early bird, the one
    who scavenges, if I am Sweeney.

Moling:

    You're mad and sly and know my name
    and recognized me. How is that?

Sweeney:

    In this enclosure time after time
    I've watched you from an airy hide-out.

Moling:

    Look at this leaf of Kevin's book,
    the coilings on this psalter's page.

Sweeney:

    The yew leaf coils around my nook
    deep in Glen Bolcain's foliage.

Moling:

    This churchyard, this whole flush of colour,
    is there no pleasure here for you?

Sweeney:

    My pleasure is great and other:
    the hosting that day at Moira.

Moling:

    I will sing Mass and make a hush
    of high celebration.

Sweeney:

    Leaping from an ivy bush
    is a higher calling even.

Moling:

    My ministry is only toil,
    the weak and strong exhaust me so.

Sweeney:

    I toil to a bed up on the chill
    steeps of Benevenagh.

Moling:

    When your end comes, is it to be
    death by water, in holy ground?

Sweeney:

    It will be early when I die.
    One of your herds will make the wound.

76 – You are more than welcome here, Sweeney, said Moling, for you are fated to live and die here. You shall leave the history of your adventures with us and receive a Christian burial in a churchyard. Therefore, said Moling, no matter how far you range over Ireland, day by day, I bind you to return to me every evening so that I may record your story.

77 All during the next year the madman kept coming back to Moling. One day he would go to Inishbofin in west Connacht, another day to lovely Assaroe. Some days he would view the clean lines of Slemish, some days he would be shivering on the Mournes. But wherever he went, every night he would be back for vespers at St Mullins.

    Moling ordered his cook to leave aside some of each day's milking for Sweeney's supper. This cook's name was Muirghil and she was married to a swineherd of Moling's called Mongan. Anyhow, Sweeney's supper was like this: she would sink her heel to the ankle in the nearest cow-dung and fill the hole to the brim with new milk. Then Sweeney would sneak into the deserted corner of the milking yard and lap it up.

78 One night there was a row between Muirghil and another woman, in the course of which the woman said:

    – If you do not prefer your husband, it is a pity you cannot take up with some other man than the looney you have been meeting all year.

    The herd's sister was within earshot and listening but she said nothing until the next morning. Then when she saw Muirghil going to leave the milk in the cow-dung beside the hedge where Sweeney roosted, she came in to her brother and said:

– Are you a man at all? Your wife's in the hedge yonder with another man.

Jealousy shook him like a brainstorm. He got up in a sudden fury, seized a spear from a rack in the house, and made for the madman. Sweeney was down swilling the milk out of the cow-dung with his side exposed towards the herd, who let go at him with the spear. It went into Sweeney at the nipple of his left breast, went through him, and broke his back.

There is another story. Some say the herd had hidden a deer's horn at the spot where Sweeney drank from the cow-dung and that Sweeney fell and killed himself on the point of it.

79 Enna McBracken was ringing the bell for prime at the door of the churchyard and saw what had happened. He spoke this poem:

80   This is sad, herd, this was deliberate,
        outrageous, sickening and sinful.
        Whoever struck here will live to regret
        killing the king, the saint, the holy fool.

        What good did you expect to come of it?
        Repentance will be denied you at your death.
        Your soul will go howling to the devil,
        your body draw an unabsolved last breath.

        But I expect to be with him in heaven,
        united in a single strain of prayer.
        The soul of the true guest is sped by psalms
        on the lips of a fasting, chanting choir.

        My heart is breaking with pity for him.
        He was a man of fame and high birth.
        He was a king, he was a madman.
        His grave will be a hallowing of earth.

81 Enna went back and told Moling that Sweeney had been killed by his swineherd Mongan. Immediately, Moling and his community came along to where Sweeney lay and Sweeney repented and made his confession to Moling. He received Christ's body and thanked God for having received it and after that was anointed by the clerics.

83 *Sweeney*:
        There was a time when I preferred
        the turtle-dove's soft jubilation
        as it flitted round a pool
        to the murmur of conversation.

        There was a time when I preferred
        the blackbird singing on the hill
        and the stag loud against the storm
        to the clinking tongue of this bell.

        There was a time when I preferred
        the mountain grouse crying at dawn
        to the voice and closeness
        of a beautiful woman.

        There was a time when I preferred
        wolf-packs yelping and howling
        to the sheepish voice of a cleric
        bleating out plainsong.

        You are welcome to pledge healths
        and carouse in your drinking dens;
        I will dip and steal water
        from a well with my open palm.

        You are welcome to that cloistered hush
        of your students' conversation;
        I will study the pure chant
        of hounds baying in Glen Bolcain.

        You are welcome to your salt meat
        and fresh meat in feasting-houses;
        I will live content elsewhere
        on tufts of green watercress.

        The herd's sharp spear wounded me
        and passed clean through my body.
        Ah Christ, who disposed all things, why
        was I not killed at Moira?

        Of all the innocent lairs I made
        the length and breadth of Ireland
        I remember an open bed
        above the lough in Mourne.

        Of all the innocent lairs I made
        the length and breadth of Ireland
        I remember bedding down
        above the wood in Glen Bolcain.

To You, Christ, I give thanks
for Your Body in communion.
Whatever evil I have done
in this world, I repent.

84 Then Sweeney's death-swoon came over him and Moling, attended by his clerics, rose up and each of them placed a stone on Sweeney's grave.

– The man who is buried here was cherished indeed, said Moling. How happy we were when we walked and talked along this path. And how I loved to watch him yonder at the well. It is called the Madman's Well because he would often eat its watercress and drink its water, and so it is named after him. And every other place he used to haunt will be cherished, too.

And then Moling said:

85 I am standing beside Sweeney's grave
remembering him. Wherever he
loved and nested and removed to
will always be dear to me.

Because Sweeney loved Glen Bolcain,
I learned to love it, too. He'll miss
all the fresh streams tumbling down,
all the beds of watercress.

He would drink his sup of water from
the well beyond that we have called
The Madman's Well; and now his name
keeps brimming in its sandy cold.

I waited long but knew he'd come.
I welcomed, sped him as a guest.
With holy viaticum
I limed him for the Holy Ghost.

Because Mad Sweeney was a pilgrim
to the lip of every well
and every green-banked, cress-topped stream,
their water's his memorial.

Now, if it be the will of God,
rise, Sweeney, take this guiding hand
that has to lay you in the sod
and draw the dark blinds of the ground.

I ask a blessing, by Sweeney's grave.
His memory rises in my breast.
His soul roosts in the tree of love.
His body sinks in its clay nest.

86 After that, Sweeney rose out of his swoon. Moling took him by the hand and both went towards the door of the church. When they reached the door Sweeney leaned his shoulders against the jamb and breathed a loud sigh. His spirit fled to heaven and his body was given an honourable burial by Moling.

87 These have been some of the stories about the adventures of Sweeney, son of Colman Cuar, king of Dal-Arie.